# 101 Ways to Meditate

Discover Your True Self

**Linda A. Lavid**

Copyright © 2014 by Linda A. Lavid
Second Edition

Without limiting the rights under copyright reserved above, no part of this publication may be reproduced, stored in or introduced into a retrieval system, or transmitted, in any form or by any means (electronic, mechanical, photocopying, recording, or otherwise), without the prior written permission of both the copyright owner and the publisher of this book.

Published by Full Court Press
A division of FCPressLLC
Buffalo, NY 14223
Website: www.fcpress.us

ISBN-10: 1499617003

ISBN-13: 978-1499617009


Printed in the United States of America
ALL RIGHTS RESERVED

# Contents

| | |
|---|---|
| Introduction... | 5 |
| Preparation... | 13 |
| Meditation Basics... | 17 |
| Processing Meditations... | 23 |
| Imagery Meditations... | 33 |
| Release Meditations... | 47 |
| Inspirational Meditations... | 65 |
| Author's Note... | 73 |
| Suggestions... | 74 |
| Meditation Journal... | 75 |
| Index of Meditations... | 139 |

## Introduction

On the day I began writing this book, I awoke with a flash of inspiration. It came a knockin' on a dull April morning in the grainy dawn light when I was half asleep trying to recall if, on the previous evening, I had brushed my teeth and locked the front door. So what was this revelation?

*You can't toss a grenade into water and call it fishing.*

At last, the answer! I then reached for a close-by journal and started a list – a list of meditations.

**Backstory...**

I'm a therapist with a Master's degree in Social Work. Over the years, I've counseled families, adults and children in agencies, hospitals, and schools. It's been a rewarding career. But five years ago my practice took a turn when I decided to explore alternative therapies. Once trained and certified, I embarked on an amazing, unexpected journey.

Before going forward, allow me to admit, I'm of a skeptical nature. I like proof of things, preferably studies and statistics with results that indicate a success rate beyond randomness. Luckily, however, I'm also of a curious nature. And so began my search.

My initial introduction to alternative therapies occurred after I went for a hypnosis session to lose weight. The session was unremarkable. I sat, closed my eyes, and listened to the hypnotherapist's voice. The script he read was pleasant but hardly earth shattering. I went home. The result: I stopped eating desserts for one full year and lost 32 pounds. It was easy, fun and very, very odd. How could 20 minutes change 55 years of sweet eating?

Turns out, hypnosis has been around for centuries, but the mechanics of how it works remains uncertain. Yes, engaging the subconscious is involved, but after that, it's a conundrum. To find the answer, I decided to be trained.

The certification course focused on hypnotherapy (hypnosis) as well as transpersonal and regression therapies. Briefly, these therapies rely on unblocking or reframing points of reference beyond the individual, that is to say *spiritual*, for positive change.

Again, this seemed odd and counterintuitive to my mathematical brain. Still, once certified, I used the skills. The result: No longer mired in circular thinking and rehashes of emotional issues, clients were able to expand their focus for true holistic change. I was shocked. What made these therapies so successful? relaxation? quieting the mind? the spiritual self? I had no idea and trekked forward.

My specialty became healing imagery. In this modality, clients define an image that represents a problem, condition, or concern, they'd like to change. It could be physical, emotional, or social. Once identified, the image is then processed. This is done by guiding the client into a relaxed state, visualizing an image, then processing it through observation and communication. Yes. The client talks to pictures inside his/her head, and I get to listen. It's fun, mysterious, and it works. The story should end here (but then there'd be no need for this book) except another challenge cropped up. Since my role was more of a facilitator than of a therapist, and the process was essentially client-driven, how could I teach myself and others to do it individually?

Seminars and research followed. I made CDs, devised hand-outs, and talked endlessly to myself and clients on how to practice solo. Unfortunately, it was ineffective. Clients' eyes glazed over and even I had trouble following my own directions.

Then that April morning the answer came:

*You can't toss a grenade into water and call it fishing.*

Eureka! Clarity amidst the morass. My complicated attempts to explain self-healing practice were overkill. Instead of using a grenade to fish, all I needed to do was simplify the process and place it in the proper vehicle. A vehicle I'd been using all along: Meditation.

## More Backstory...

My excursions into meditation were also roundabout. Having been raised and educated in an environment heavily saturated with dogma and a certain way of doing things, meditation was of another world, foreign and vaguely blasphemous. It was the early seventies and Eastern religions, thanks to the Beatles, were hot. I started yoga and meditation.

The yoga was easy since Lilias was on PBS, but the meditation practice was hazy. No one seemed to know exactly how it was done or what to expect. From readings, it seemed like it was about nothing. So that's what I did – thought about nothing.

For three months, I spent 45 minutes a day doing yoga and meditation. Two positive things happened: muscles loosened and insights floated unexpectedly into my mind. But there was a problem – 45 minutes became overwhelming. I had to work, pay bills, and couldn't swing it. Result: Muscles stiffened. Thoughts clouded. And soon I was back to my old self.

Over the years, I returned to yoga and meditative practice, but never for long periods of time. What can I say? It always came down to time, its restrictions, and, I'm ashamed to admit, it was…well…rather boring. Years passed.

My next exposure to meditation came from a visit I made to Lily Dale, a spiritualist community in upstate New York. My purpose there was to be in calm surroundings to write. It's a safe and kindly place for a retreat. During the summer season, part of the daily programming includes a meditation service held in the small chapel at 8 AM. I thought it would be a nice way to start my writing day.

From the first moment, it felt like I had come home. Outside leaves rustled, birds chirped. Inside, jewel-toned stained glass glowed in flickering candlelight. I closed my eyes, breathed deeply, and for 25 minutes I was transported. Part of me was present and aware. Another part felt sacred. I returned each day. By week's end, I finally realized how to make meditation enjoyable. Rather than the Spartan approach of stretching and thinking of nothing, I needed some razzle dazzle.

I continued practicing healing imagery on clients and meditating on my own. There were points (setting the stage with sound, light, scent) of commonality, but the practices differed. One was personal and spiritual. The other was professional and dealt with imagery. The melding of the two occurred that April morning when I clearly understood that the tenets of meditation were the same as healing imagery. It wasn't just the relaxation of mind and body, but of the focus. Specifically, whether you are experiencing nothing or experiencing something, you are meditating. And *101 Ways to Meditate* was born.

So what exactly is meditation? In the simplest of terms, it's about relaxing the body, quieting the mind, and having a focus. It's also a way to access knowledge intuitively, to experience a world beyond the senses, to communicate with the personal or collective unconscious and, most importantly, to understand who you are.

Before going further, I'd like to say, other than relaxing the body, mind and having a focus, there is no right or wrong way to meditate. Whatever works for you is the right way. Meditation is personal and accommodates itself to your frame of reference and choice of focus.

Why meditate? We all have so many questions: Who am I? Why am I here? Why do I behave the way I do? And, to answer these questions, we search by observing, reasoning, experimenting. Still no matter how many answers come our way, more questions remain. I suspect if life were clear and easily divined, the mystery and intrigue of living would quickly bore us and we'd shrivel up. We are meant to question, to search. It's in our DNA. But there are other reasons to meditate.

Meditation heals at every level. Physically, a meditative state: releases toxins, relieves stress, enhances relaxation, improves heart/lung efficiency, increases energy, reduces fatigue, and increases oxygen throughout the body. For emotional wounds, psychological trauma, meditation is a soothing balm and an accommodating resource to release unneeded baggage. Finally, to make sense of the chaos – at times ego-produced, at times out of our hands – meditation helps us step back and take a grander perspective beyond the personal.

Meditation is versatile. Gone are my days of facing 45 minutes of practice that often seemed too removed from everyday life. Meditation is a way to explore and understand the great mysteries, but it's also a way to understand yourself. Answers to questions big and small can occur with any meditation. In fact, you may meditate for one reason, but a breakthrough may come in another area. Example: Perhaps you're meditating to release anger when a week later you unceremoniously toss out that last pack of cigarettes.

Finally, meditation is fun, exciting, and always new. Razzle and dazzle of the highest order. For this, you'll just have to try.

**About this book...**

## Introduction

I've divided the meditations into four
Processing, Imagery, Release, and Inspiration
group has a different focus although, at times, the boundaries blur. You may find an affinity toward one block of meditations or you may want to mix it up. My wish is to briefly describe a wide selection of meditations so you can try different ways of meditating to see what works best. Alas, we learn differently, have varied preferences, and one size does not fit all. Once you become comfortable with meditative practice, you'll be able to put together meditations of your own. In fact, *101 Ways to Meditate* will only be a starting point.

**Processing Meditations** are traditional ways of meditating. They are used to gain knowledge and understanding of God, divine purpose, or higher awareness. Processing Meditations focus on relaxing the body and quieting the mind.

**Imagery Meditations** focus on images that can be seen, heard, smelled, felt, and/or sensed. Imagery Meditations help with gaining a greater understanding of the subconscious state by using the intermediary language of imagery, memory, emotion and/or metaphor.

**Release Meditations** focus on negative emotions and their release. Images, often in the form of metaphors, denote underlying emotions that are then processed. Release Meditations clear the body and mind of toxicity.

**Inspirational Meditations** explore spiritual or transpersonal issues using imagery as their focus. Inspirational Meditations add color and texture to the otherwise somber Processing Meditations.

Beyond the listing of meditations, is a 31-day journal to keep track of your progress and document the wonder that awaits. For easy reference, a full listing of all the meditations can be found in the index.

I hope I have intrigued you into trying or expanding meditative practice. If so, gather your unfettered curiosity, highest intention, rip-roaring enthusiasm, and let's begin.

## Preparation

Synchronizing your body and mind for meditative practice involves setting the proper environment for yourself and your surroundings.

**Preparing yourself:**

- Perform in a safe environment.
- Wear relaxed clothing.
- Attend to bathroom needs prior to practice.
- Maintain a comfortable temperature.
- Do not be too hungry or full.
- Position yourself comfortably.
- Reduce distractions.
- Have tissues handy.

Think about a time when you walked into a place of worship and lit a votive candle; or when you turned down the lights and listened to music; or took a long walk on a beach. However you were able to buffer the outer world and ease into a familiar calm is how meditation should be approached. Ideas for preparing your environment are listed below. Try them on for size. It's not necessary to do them all. Pick, choose, or go out on your own.

**Preparing your environment:**

- **Set up an altar.** An altar is a reminder of the ritual, which in turn, prepares your body and mind for practice. Place objects in your sacred place that have meaning for you.

- **Have a mantra.** Historically mantras are assigned to an individual by a spiritual teacher. A mantra is a sound that creates spiritual transformation. A commonly used mantra is Ohm or Aum. Developing a comfortable mantra of your own is fine as well. Play around with single-syllable sounds that feel pleasing to you. Mantras can be spoken aloud or silently. They should be connected to the breath on the inhale and exhale.

- **Add an affirmation or prayer.** When adding an affirmation (positive thought) or prayer, think of the mood you want to set. An affirmation and/or prayer can be lifted from religious texts or made up by you. Options are many and varied. Use those that have significant meaning for you and set a receptive tone.

- **Use Beads.** For counting repetitions, consider using prayer beads, a rosary, or any number of items you can string together: seashells, legumes, beads from broken jewelry, etc. The advantage of making your own strand is that you can customize the number of beads. Example: I use counts of 40 for my breathing meditation induction.

- **Light a candle.** Candles fill an area with calming soft light. One-hundred percent (no blends) beeswax or soy candles with lead-free wicks are the friendliest to the environment and to your lungs. LED candles are safe alternatives.

- **Scent.** Incense, scented candles, plug-ins, flowers, can be used for focus, to soothe, or to encourage breathing. Care should be taken when using essential oils since they are concentrated and, depending on the oil, potentially toxic.

- **Sound.** Nature sounds, music, Tibetan bowls, chimes, even playing a wind instrument (long exhales calm the body) help a meditative session. An advantage of using taped sounds is that you can arrange the sounds to fill the length of your meditation session. This way you don't have to keep glancing at the clock.

There are many ways, only limited by your imagination, to prepare for a session. Busy schedules, family/work lives, space issues, may have to be taken into account. Still, a way can be found to set aside a place and time, even if it's in bed, when you awaken or go to sleep.

## Meditation Basics

Cornerstones of the meditative process are simple but important. The following tenets will assure success. As you read what follows, understand that each step, even journaling, plays off the other like an orchestrated ensemble of blended notes. In other words, the practice of meditation is not linear but dynamic. For instance, relaxing the body can be a focus that can then quiet the mind, which then allows for more focus.

**Allow 20 minutes.** Meditation is not ego-driven, that is to say, the thinking brain does not drive the meditative experience. Meditation is a communication with our intuitive, transpersonal, subconscious selves. To do this, the body and mind must be relaxed and remain in an impersonal, receptive state. It takes most people 7 to 10 minutes to quiet their bodies and minds. The remainder of the time is for focusing. Once meditation is practiced regularly, you may be able to relax your body and mind more quickly. Still, it's advisable to meditate for the full 20 minutes. Consistent shortening of the meditation time, can lead to a daydream state rather than a meditative state, which in turn may sabotage all the benefits meditation has to offer.

**Set the tone.** Consider the following words: compassionate, playful, acknowledging, open, curious, hopeful, receptive, allowing, accepting, surrendering. These words express the tone by which a meditative session becomes fertile. Setting a receptive tone can be done with an affirmation, prayer, image, or how the environment is staged (see page 14.) Example: Before I meditate, I light a candle, put on a CD, and visualize a budding red rose. Receptivity can also be expressed during meditation.

**Relax the body.** The body cruises along on its own, or at least that's what we were taught in school. Don't believe it. Trillions of cells, endless maneuverings, sparks of electrical energy are bombarded by memories, stress, toxins, diseases that lock into tissues, bones, muscles, organs, nerves, etc., throwing off our natural ability to be balanced. So how can we settle our bodies down? By breathing, slowly and deeply. This is done by elongating exhales and breathing from the diaphragm, that part around your belly button. In the Processing Meditation section, you'll find many ways to relax your body. Try different ones to see which work best. Breathing alone can be a meditation that heals body, mind and spirit.

**Clear the mind.** To explore subterranean places, one needs to cut the distractions. A ticker tape replay of the day's highs and lows, worries about this and that, anger, judgment, fear, anxiety, negative self-talk have to stop. It's all static. Imagine trying to listen to a ball game at a rock concert. Before long, frustration settles in and you give up. Processing Meditations often focus on clearing all thought. This is done by focusing on how muscles move, how the breath is taken, or in the absorption of a simple sensory detail such as a ticking clock. As in relaxing the body, clearing the mind can be a meditation on its own.

**Develop a focus.** The focus is the core of the meditation. Each of the 101 meditations listed has a core component (focus) that is explained in its description. The focus of a meditation is the key that unlocks mysteries. Surprise and insight may occur during this period as the boundaries of the intuitive, subconscious or spiritual states become permeable. It is often through metaphor, imagery, memory, and emotion that insight is able to bubble into our conscious minds. When unusual images present themselves, pay attention, examine their detail, then dialogue. Should tears arise, allow them to flow for when there are tears, of joy or sorrow, there is truth.

**Give gratitude.** Gratitude is a powerful tool in meditation because it honors and thanks the process. Whatever your wellspring of universal wisdom (healing energy, higher power, your subconscious) happens to be, it needs to be thanked. But there's another reason. By giving gratitude, you also show an openness to receive, which in turn encourages your wellspring of wisdom to give more. Think of how it feels to receive a sincere thank you from someone. How likely would you be to give again? Expressing gratitude communicates this and can be done throughout or at the end of a meditative session.

**Journal.** Journaling is an account of your meditative session, a blueprint for future meditations, and another way to acknowledge and thank the process. The best time to journal is right after the session while the experience is fresh. Reviewing the meditation can lead to greater clarity since your mind is on track and ready to evaluate. In summarizing your meditative experience, document: content, images and insights gained; what made you happy or sad; the meditation used and its effectiveness; any problems with relaxing the body, clearing the mind and/or keeping focus. After evaluating the journal entry, you can plan future action. How can you tweak the meditation to make it more effective? What threads need to be revisited for greater understanding? By taking the time to journal, you are honoring and thanking the process by giving it attention beyond the actual meditation. This in turn will lead to greater pans of gold. While at times, meditation can be a process of fits and starts, it's also a practice that builds on itself. Journaling is an integral part of establishing a solid foundation. A 31-day journal is included in this book. Use it as you see fit.

## On Meditation Block...

No matter how well you prepare, how great your intention, how open you are to the process, on some days, your meditative practice may be ineffective, boring, frustrating.

Here are some possible blocks and how to address them.

- **Intrusive thoughts**. After some attempts to bring yourself back, give gratitude and gently awake. Once fully alert, write down what was so intrusive. Were these thoughts a rehash of the day or wildly tangential? If the former, try a different meditation; if the latter, document in journal, and evaluate how these thoughts can become a focus for another day's meditation.

- **Fall asleep.** Change the position you're in and/or change aspects of environment, i.e., play different music. If you still fall asleep, perhaps you're genuinely tired and need to get some rest.

- **Rushing through.** Not allowing at least 20 minutes of meditative time will eventually short-circuit and sabotage the process. Consider having a guest for dinner who's always looking at his watch. Is he encouraging interaction? enjoying the food? expressing gratitude? And, most importantly, will you invite him back?

- **Body too wired.** Not everyone can lie or sit down and relax. If you tend to be very active, begin with a moving or walking Processing Meditation.

- **Nothing's happening.** Ask yourself if there is an underlying resistance to meditation. Could your upbringing, religious background, belief system be affecting your practice?

- **Fearful of not doing it right.** Be kind to yourself. However you can navigate and make meditative practice worthwhile is what's important. There are no tests; no one's watching. Be playful.

Wizened and prepared for meditative practice, it's now time for the 101 ways...

## Processing Meditations

A Processing Meditation is a basic, sometimes traditional, style of meditation. Processing Meditations often use focal points of breathing, chanting, being in the moment, sitting in a certain position, and are less directed toward specific images or thoughts. Processing Meditations prime your body, mind, and spirit to be receptive to subconscious and unconscious states by relaxing the body, quieting the mind, and bringing forth a tone of allowing. These meditations, in an abbreviated form of 7 to 10 minutes (an induction), are also used in preparation for Imagery, Release, and Inspirational Meditations.

Consider a Processing Meditation like floating on your back absorbing the sun in a warm pool of water. Note the calm and receptiveness this image portrays. Processing Meditations increase receptiveness to other states of awareness.

An aside...

Many religions use meditation and/or prayer as integral parts of their practice. As nomadic groups, religious sects migrated the world, meditation and prayer often took on different names. Still, the basic practice remained the same. In the meditations that follow, please understand it is not my intention to minimize or marginalize certain religious practices.

**Meditation Basics:**
- **Put aside twenty minutes.**
- **Set a receptive tone.**
- **Relax your body.**
- **Clear your mind.**
- **Focus.**
- **Give gratitude.**
- **Journal.**

1. **Relaxation Meditation** – A relaxed body is necessary for all meditative practice. Therefore this type of meditation, shortened (an induction), is commonly used no matter what kind of meditation you are doing. In this meditation, make yourself comfortable, close your eyes, and take abdominal breaths. By placing your hand on your lower belly, you should feel your diaphragm move up and down. This is an abdominal breath. Breaths should be comfortable. With effortless, circular breathing, relax your body. Begin from the top of your head and work down slowly. Imagine your muscles relaxing from your head, neck, shoulders and beyond. If there is any tightness, relax those muscles. If you don't know if your muscles are tight or loose, contract then loosen them. Stress often can be found in the jaw, neck, and shoulders. This meditation is simply about becoming more relaxed. Once you

have relaxed every muscle, simply float and drift. **Focus: Relaxing muscles.**

2. **Breath Meditation** – A breath meditation is being aware of each breath taken. To begin this meditation, relax your body (see above.) Once your muscles are loose, begin by concentrating on your breath. While there are no hard and fast rules, a longer exhale helps to deepen the meditation. To further focus on the breath, listen to the way it sounds when released from your nose (preferably) or mouth. Should pain or discomfort arise in any part of your body, stay on the edge of it and gently release it through the breath. Cleansing the body of toxins is an added benefit of breath work. **Focus: The breath.**

3. **4-4-8 Meditation** – This is a breathing meditation that is counted. To the count of 4, inhale deeply. For 4 counts, hold breath. To the count of 8, exhale. Do 3 sets of 12 repetitions, or 36 times. Add more sets as preferred. This meditation can also be used as an induction for other meditations. Keep track of repetitions with beads. **Focus: Counting.**

4. **Mindful of the Moment (Mindfulness) Meditation** – Once relaxed, select a focal point from the environment and contemplate it. Imagine that you are experiencing this detail for the first time. Absorb the nuances. Should intrusive thoughts draw you away, gently refocus back to the focal point. Focal points can be

external (ticking of a clock) or internal (pressure point of feet on floor.) Mindfulness can also be performed in a fully awaken state (a walk in the park with particular attention to chirping birds.) Studies indicate after six weeks of performing a daily mindfulness meditation, anxiety levels decreased and immune function improved. **Focus: A sensory detail.**

5. **Prayer Meditation** – Begin by quieting the mind and relaxing the body. Once relaxed, recite a prayer that has special meaning for you. Repeat aloud or in your mind. Feel the power of the prayer as it emanates from thought through expression. **Focus: A prayer.**

6. **Word Repetition Meditation** – Relax with a breath or relaxation meditation, then repeat, aloud or silently, a mantra (Ohm, Aum) or self-selected word. Allow the repeated sequence to become part of your breath, on the inhale and exhale. When intrusive thoughts occur, gently refocus. Repetition Meditations are good for those who need sound to relax. Mantras are usually assigned by spiritual teachers, but any pleasing word can also be used. Single-syllable words are good choices. Notice the vibrational quality as the word is stretch out during an exhale. For a specific longer mantra, see Kundalini Mantra Meditation #17. **Focus: Sound repetition.**

7. **Body Scan Meditation** – Relax with a breath or relaxation meditation, then begin to scan your

body starting wherever you choose. For instance, if you are sitting in a chair, feel your spine as it rests against the chair back. Body scans do not rest on one spot but move along the entire body. Just notice how that part feels, accept the sensation, and move along to a connected section. In other words, you could start with your right foot, then go to your right ankle, then move up your right leg. Studies have showed that patients with chronic pain have benefited from doing body scans. **Focus: A body scan.**

8. **Taoist Meditation** – Relax and breathe. Once calm and mind is clear, focus on the breath, but instead of it coming and going through the nose, imagine it entering the body from a spot on the crown of the head, two inches up from the center hairline. With the inhale, feel the energy enter the body and travel down the spine to below the navel, then as you exhale have the breath circle its way up the spine to be released from the same spot. When the breath and energy are exhaled, the spot may feel as if a flap or valve is opening up. Scalp may become warm, tingling, or numb during the process. **Focus: A breath traveling through the body.**

9. **Draw Breath to Parts of the Body Meditation** – Relax and Breathe. When mind is clear, draw the inhaled breath to any part of the body that needs healing energy. Should there be any pain during the meditation, stay on the edge of it and continue to allow the healing energy of the

breath to wash over, around, and through the area. A session can be spent on one area or multiple spots. **Focus: Breaths to parts of body that need healing.**

10. **Reduce Chatter Meditation** – This is a meditation as well as a technique to release intrusive thoughts that may be preventing you from focusing. As thoughts go rogue and rush through your mind, mentally, at one end of your brain, close a door. With no outlet, experience the stream of consciousness dam up in a sea of tumbling words, phrases. When your head is full, open the door and let it all rush out. **Focus: Blockage and release.**

11. **Walking Meditation** – This meditation takes place while you are awake and walking. Once calm, focus on the act of walking beginning with the sensation of your feet on the ground. Slowly move up your body and acknowledge the bones, muscles, tendons, organs involved in performing this everyday activity. **Focus: Walking.**

12. **Loving Kindness Meditation** – Relax, breathe and when ready, tap into the feeling of love. Think of a loved person or pet, then focus on the feeling this gives you in your heart chakra, the center of your chest. Once the feeling is strong, extend it outward to the universe. This extension of love can be sent to specific people, both the ones you love and those not so loveable.
**Focus: Feeling of love.**

13. **Not-Trying Meditation** – This meditation, reminiscent of reverse psychology, is comparable to not thinking of an elephant. When ready to meditate: try not to breathe deeply, try not to quiet your thoughts, try not to be comfortable, try not to be in the present, try not to empty your mind, try not to be open, try not to be compassionate, try not to surrender, try not to meditate for 20 minutes. (Of course the goal is to do all of the above.) **Focus: To not try.**

14. **Inner Sound Meditation** – Relax, clear your mind, and, if necessary, use earplugs. Listen to the sounds inside your body, i.e., your breath, heartbeat, whooshing of blood in your head. Some sounds may lead to others. If you can't hear any sounds, simply keep open. When a sound is particularly pleasant, give it more attention. **Focus: Inner body sounds.**

15. **Inner Light/Screen Meditation** – When your mind is clear and body is relaxed, focus on the inner screen behind your eyelids. What do you see? With calm attention stay focused. Perhaps lighter patches will appear. As you fall into a greater meditative state, the area may become darker. With calm awareness return your attention to where there were different tones of color including grays. Remain focused. **Focus: Colors seen with closed eyes.**

16. **Chakra Meditation** – A meditation for Chakras can include drawing healing white light to each

energy center or increasing the light/color of that energy center. Chakras are seven energy areas within your body. Each energy field has a light or color associated with it. Briefly, the centers and colors are: Base of the spine (red); Below the navel (orange); Solar Plexus around diaphragm area (yellow); Heart (green); Throat (medium blue); Third Eye above the eyes (indigo); Crown of Head (violet). When body and mind are calm, imagine drawing a healing white light to each Chakra. Experience how this affects the color of the Chakra. **Focus: Healing light to Chakra areas.**

17. **Kundalini Mantra Meditation** – Sit with your spine straight. Breathe, relax, and once your mind is clear, say aloud or in your mind the following healing mantra: Ra Ma Da Sa Say So Hung. The meaning of each syllable is: Ra (sun), Ma (moon), Da (earth), Sa (totality), Say (infinity), So (self), Hung (divine). **Focus: Mantra.**

18. **Inner Smile Meditation** – Breathe, relax. Once calm and free from thought, gently contemplate what a smile feels like. To do this you can think of some person or thing that makes you smile. You can also turn up the corners of your lips into a pleasant smile. Once this feeling of acceptance and love is sensed, allow it into your body through your third eye (forehead area) and allow it to smile to any part of your body that needs

kind energy. The Inner Smile helps to live in harmony with yourself. **Focus: A smile.**

19. **Movement Meditation** – This meditation is for those who find that movement relaxes them. Stand into a relaxed position and visualize drawing energy from the earth. With or without music, gently move in anyway that pleases you, i.e., open like a flower, move like a cat, dance. Whatever area of the body is tight, allow movement to loosen it. **Focus: Movement.**

20. **Laughing Buddha Meditation** – This meditation is a waking meditation that was started in Japan by a man who visited towns and performed in the square by only laughing. He was revered and loved. To begin, relax your body, mind, and turn the corners of your lips into a smile. Follow this with laughter, or Ha-Has. Feel how the energy in your body changes. **Focus: Laughter.**

21. **Stretching Meditation** – This meditation is a movement meditation. Eyes can be open or closed. Breathe easily and keep focus on how muscles feel when stretched. Yoga's Sun Salutation or Tai Chi 24 are types of stretching meditations. If you are unfamiliar with these exercises, simply make up a routine of your own. Do not strain. Try to make movements, slow and fluid, feeling how the muscles stretch and relax. Take breaths naturally depending on your body movements. **Focus: Stretching muscles.**

## Imagery Meditations

An Imagery Meditation uses imagery as its focus. Imagery can be anything that is: seen, heard, smelled, tasted, felt. Images or sensory data can be considered before the meditation or arise spontaneously during the meditation. To begin an Imagery Meditation, start with a basic Processing Meditation, i.e., Breath Meditation for 7 to 10 minutes. To get the most out of an Imagery Meditation, it's best to have a relaxed body and clear mind. This softens the boundary between your conscious and subconscious mind.

Imagery Meditations are powerful tools to communicate with the subconscious. While dreams are a one-way conversation from the subconscious to you, imagery is a two-way discussion utilizing the intermediary language of memories, emotions, symbols, metaphors and images.

Imagery Meditations help you gain insight into your behavior which, in turn, can free you up for personal and spiritual growth. Many of the meditations listed also call for dialogue or processing. In these cases, you are encouraged to speak with the image, express any questions, concerns, feelings and listen to its response.

**Meditation Basics:**

- **Put aside twenty minutes.**
- **Set a receptive tone.**
- **Relax your body.**
- **Clear your mind.**
- **Focus.**
- **Give gratitude.**
- **Journal.**

22. **Special Place Meditation** – Relax, breathe and when your mind is blank imagine a peaceful, special place. It can be from a memory, created spontaneously, or be a mixture of the two. Special places can be changed or edited at any time. Pay attention to details, such as light, temperature, or sensations. Comforting and safe, this meditation can be revisited often. Symbols, images and feelings from the subconscious are sure to arise, which can then be explored during other meditations. **Focus: Special place.**

23. **Details from a Special Place Meditation** – Relax, breathe and when your mind is clear, revisit your special place and focus on any detail that is particularly interesting or pleasing. It could be an animal, a plant, a rock, a color, a smell, even another person. Remember it's through images, symbols, metaphors, emotions that the subconscious communicates to us. When an image or sensory detail appears, act as

though you're meeting it in real life. Introduce yourself and have a conversation. Afterwards, jot down notes in your journal. Guides, totem animals, angels, wise ones, religious figures, to name a few, can reveal themselves in your special place. Yes, and they can be revisited as often as you like. **Focus: Special place detail with dialogue.**

24. **Pet Meditation** – Relax your body and mind. Once ready, bring forth a favorite pet, alive or deceased. Experience the presence of this animal in vivid detail. When ready, look deeply in this animal's eyes, knowing it is full of love and acceptance. What advice does it have for you? What can you do for it? Dialogue. **Focus: Favorite pet.**

25. **Totem Animal Meditation** – A totem animal, once established, can be a support when doing other types of meditation. A totem animal can be taken from your everyday life. For instance, do you hold an affinity toward one type of animal? Do you collect animal figurines? Another way of finding a totem animal is if it appears in another type of meditation (Special Place Meditation #22.) Yet a third way is to call forth a totem animal during any meditative session. Initially, the image may not be fully developed. In other words, the image could be a scent, sound, impression, etc. Whenever an image is sensed, acknowledge it and start a conversation. Why did it pick you? What does it want to tell you? What can you do for it? The more a totem animal is

fleshed out, the more you'll understand it and your relationship. **Focus: Totem animal.**

26. **Enjoy a Bountiful Moment Meditation** – Once your body and mind are relaxed, imagine a moment that makes you feel wonderful. It can be a recollection or something imagined. Experience this moment as vividly as possible. Use all of your senses. How does your body and mind respond? Extend this moment for the entire meditative session. **Focus: Bountiful moment.**

27. **Drop of Rain Meditation** – Once your mind is clear and your body is relaxed, experience an element, creature, event in the natural world. The possibilities are unlimited...a drop of rain as it forms then falls from the sky; a squirrel as it forages the ground then climbs the tree. Become this element and absorb the experience it has. **Focus: Perspective of event from nature.**

28. **Open Doors Meditation** – Calm your body and mind and when ready imagine a hallway of doors in front of you. When ready, go to a door and open it. What do you see, hear, sense? Be curious or shut the door. If a question arises, ask it. Should you sense trepidation, simply stay on the edge of the feeling or call in a totem animal (Totem Animal Meditation #25), wise one (Wise One Meditation #84), saint (Saint Meditation #100) to be by your side. **Focus: Opening a door.**

## Imagery Meditations

29. **Gift Meditation** – Relax, calm your body and mind. When ready, imagine selecting a present for someone and giving to him/her. You may have a gift and person in mind or you may spontaneously select a gift and give it to a stranger. Example: Pick flowers in a field, then approach a house. Knock on the door and give the flowers to whomever answers. There may or may not be a conversation. Should emotions arise, allow them. **Focus: Giving a gift.**

30. **Sit in Nature Meditation** – This is a waking meditation. Go into an outdoor area that is pleasing to you. Breathe, relax and when you are ready, focus your attention on a detail of the landscape. Look, listen, touch, smell, sense this detail from every aspect. Contemplate how this object can connect and heal you. Example: You may select the waves as they roll onto the shore. What is healing about this? Perhaps, after contemplation, you understand how water cleanses rock, or how receding waves take away debris. **Focus: Healing nature.**

31. **Seed Planting Meditation** – Relax and calm your body and mind. Imagine before you a display of seed packets. There are hundreds of packets. All are guaranteed to grow. Look over the packets, what calls your attention? Select one and look at the packet. What is the seed called? What are the instructions? If you like, plant these seeds and watch what happens. **Focus: Planting seeds.**

32. **Question Meditation** – Before beginning, write down a question in your journal for which you want an answer. Once your mind is clear and your body is relaxed do any Processing Meditation (Breath Meditation #2), or relaxing meditation (Special Place Meditation #22.) You may think of the question lightly or let it sit in the background. Answer may come during meditation or afterwards when you journal. **Focus: A question.**

33. **Performance Meditation** – Once your body is relaxed and your mind is clear, imagine in detail, a task, sport, activity that you'd like to improve upon. Experience the place, time of day, temperature, sound, colors in vivid detail. Embedded to the moment, focus on the task at hand. Breathe, easily and effortlessly, as you initiate and complete the performance. If you like, successfully execute this activity over again or in different ways. **Focus: Successful completion of a task.**

34. **Spontaneous Image Meditation** – After quieting your mind and body, imagine sitting in a darkened theater. On the stage is a blank screen. When ready, allow an image to play on the screen. To clarify the image, turn the controls located on the armrest. The image could be a symbol or something ordinary. It also could be a smell, a sound, a taste, a feeling. Once the image is clear, tell the image how you feel about it. Allow it to respond. Ask the image what it wants from you. Allow it to respond. The importance or

meaning of this image may or may not be clear at first. Document in journal. **Focus: Image on screen.**

35. **Grounding Meditation** – After your body is relaxed and your mind is clear, imagine a healing light (however you sense it) entering the crown of your head. Experience this healing energy as it enters your heart then radiates through muscles, nerves, organs, bones. Experience this energy passing down your legs into your feet and beyond. Sense this energy then travel deeply into the ground through layers of earth and stone until it enters the molten center of the earth where more energy is gathered to climb up through the layers of rock and dirt until it reenters your body, to then reunite with your heart's center. **Focus: Healing energy.**

36. **Body Celebration Meditation** – Relax your body and mind. When ready, carefully observe your body image from a detached position. From the top of your head to your toes, acknowledge what is pleasing about this body. Is it strong, resilient? Does it have attractive features? When ready go inside this body. What is good about this body on the inside? Which part is healthy, useful? Finally, observe how this body has helped, pleased, and given you life on earth. **Focus: Body Acknowledgement.**

37. **Kindness Meditation** – Relax your body and clear your mind. When ready imagine yourself at home on a rainy, cold, moonless night. There's a

knock on the door. Upon opening the door, find a person, animal, object that is in need. Do whatever comes naturally, i.e., ask questions, try to help, give it love and understanding. **Focus: Kindness.**

38. **Success Meditation** – When body is relaxed and your mind is clear, imagine some of the goals you have achieved and the positive events that have graced your life. Take one goal and look at it closely. Review how you reached that goal and how it affected you, your family, friends, and/or people you worked with. Breathe and feel how reaching this goal felt. Imagine achieving newer goals. What steps need to be taken? **Focus: Steps to success.**

39. **Healing Meditation** – Research has documented successful healing of disease by engaging the imagination. Studies have also shown that a person does not have to understand how the illness has manifested in the body for the visualization to work. Relax, clear your mind and call an image forward that could help you return to a healthful state. Experience the image as it works to rid your body of disease. Release Meditations found on page 59 address specific health conditions. **Focus: Healing image.**

40. **Letting Go Meditation** – Once your body is relaxed and your mind is calm, imagine letting go of an unwanted feeling or thought that is locked in your body or mind. Be still and observe this feeling or thought. When ready, exhale this

feeling or thought into a balloon. When the balloon is full, allow the balloon to rise up and away from you. Imagine it getting smaller as it rises toward the clouds and sky, until *poof*, it's gone. **Focus: Letting go of an unwanted feeling or thought.**

41. **Protector Meditation** – Inside us all is a protector. It may take many forms. The protector guards us against injury, hurt, pain. The protector, when too watchful, can also cause problems, like an overly protective parent. Relax your body and mind. When ready, call forth your protector. The presence can be an image, a smell, a taste, a sound, a feeling. Accept whatever comes and dialogue by ask questioning, listening, and expressing concerns. **Focus: Dialogue with a protector.**

42. **Adjustment Meditation** – Relax and breathe easily. Allow your mind to become quiet. When ready, imagine an area inside you that is a control center. Enter that area and look at the control panel where functions of your body are set. There are levers, switches, knobs, dials of many kinds. Should you wish to adjust a setting, look for its label (i.e. metabolism) and adjust the lever, switch, knob, dial to the ideal setting for your body. Once an adjustment is made, allow your body to respond. **Focus: Settings in your body.**

43. **Pre-Surgery Meditation** – When relaxed, imagine a special place that is comforting and

safe. Experience this place in detail. What aspect of this special place feels to be the most calming and healing? When ready, reduce this detail to a cue of one or two words. Example: If a comforting place is a beach, you might think of calm waters. The cue would then be *calm waters.* Prior to surgery, should anxiety arise, think of your cue word(s): *calm waters*. **Focus: Cue word(s).**

44. **Post-Surgery Meditation** – This meditation can begin in recovery. Once your eyes are open, gently scan the room and find an object (light, temperature, flowers) that is pleasing. As you absorb this object's detail repeat your cue words from the Pre-Surgery Meditation. When calmed and comforted, imagine, in detail, how your body is beginning to heal. Allow breaths to relax and comfort you. **Focus: Cue words and healing imagery.**

45. **Childbirth Meditation** – Relax, clear your mind and when ready draw forth your special place, a place that is comfortable and safe. Enjoy the sights, sounds, and general sense of the place. Breathe easily and effortlessly. When calm, communicate your feelings, dreams and hopes to your baby. Allow your baby to communicate back. **Focus: Special place and dialogue with baby.**

46. **Departed One Meditation** – Relax, clear your mind and, when ready, draw forth a departed one. Welcome this person with openness. Have a

conversation. Ask questions, express feelings and clear emotions with understanding, forgiveness and love. **Focus: Conversation with a departed one.**

The following meditations explore how different parts of you are doing. Delineating aspects of yourself, help clarify where issues and concerns are. Each meditation may bring forth other areas to work on.

47. **Physical Body Meditation** – When relaxed and mind is clear, from a detached position, imagine looking at your physical body. Do a quick scan of your physical body, inside and out. Is your overall health good? Do you sense any problems, issues, complaints? What does the body need? Can you provide this? **Focus: Detached view of body.**

48. **Emotional Body Meditation** – When relaxed and mind is clear, from a detached position, imagine looking at your emotional body. An emotional body is your feeling, emotional self. Sense the state of your emotional wellness. Are there particular problematic feelings, somatic complaints, or troubling images that come forth? If so, what can you do to bring health to this emotional body? Take action. **Focus: Detached view of emotional body.**

49. **Intellectual Body Meditation** – When relaxed and mind is clear, from a detached position, imagine looking at your intellectual body. Does this intellectual body appear weak in any way?

What does this thinking body need that will restore it to health? Provide whatever it needs to return it to wellness and vitality. **Focus: Detached view of intellectual body.**

50. **Spiritual Body Meditation** – Relax, breathe, and when ready, call forth your spiritual self. This spiritual self can come through as an image, a taste, a smell, a sound, or a sense. What is it like to be in the presence of your spiritual self? Does it have a message or gift for you? Whatever is presented, accept it with loving kindness. If you have any questions, ask them. **Focus: Your spiritual self.**

51. **Integration Meditation** – With a relaxed and clear mind, bring forth your physical, emotional, intellectual, spiritual bodies in the same place. When ready, merge these bodies into the self. Once blended together, sense the state of your integrated self. How balanced is it? What can you do to make it strong and whole? **Focus: Integration of separate parts.**

Tucked inside all of us, and for better or worse, are events that have changed us. Accessing these memories and reprocessing or releasing them can help improve the quality of our lives. Memory meditations excavate past places, events, people and can be pondered as often as you like. Should emotions arise, gently release them.

52. **Simple Memory Meditation** – A simple memory is a memory that has, ostensibly, little or no

emotional content. Breathe, relax and clear your mind. When ready, draw forward a specific time or place to remember. It could be long ago or more recent. Example: Recall your bedroom as a child. When you first begin, you may only remember a couple of things, but as you continue to inhabit the area, more details will surface. Since memories are not stored in one part of the brain, doing simple memory meditations help with recall and the ability to visualize. Should an emotion surface, stay on the edge of it and allow it to be released. **Focus: A non-specific memory.**

53. **Favorite Memory Meditation** – Breathe, relax and clear your mind of clutter. When ready, draw forth a favorite memory. Experience the memory from different sensory inputs, i.e., what you see, hear, smell, feel. Then consider looking at yourself from different perspectives, as if you're on a movie screen. Should a feeling arise, stay on the edge of it and allow it to be released. **Focus: A favorite memory.**

54. **Pivotal Memory Meditation** – A pivotal memory is a memory that may elicit uncomfortable feelings. When feelings come up, stay on the edge of them. If they can be released, do so. When a memory is painful and unable to be process, gently wish it well and slowly awaken. Pivotal memories can be revisited often. You can simply watch the screen with the knowledge that you are removed, safe and in control. A totem animal (Totem Animal

Meditation #25) or wise one (Wise One Meditation #84) can be called forth to help navigate the event. **Focus: Processing an emotional memory.**

55. **Inner Child Meditation** – Relax, breathe easily, and when your mind is clear, bring to the fore yourself as a child. It can be at any age. Welcome this image, impression, or energy that appears. You can observe the child or have a conversation with it, i.e., introduce yourself and ask there is anything the child needs from you. Be playful. If an uncomfortable emotion comes up, stay on the edge of it, and allow it to be released. If a joyful or calm feeling arises, hold it closer. **Focus: Yourself as a child.**

## Release Meditations

Release Meditations are similar to Imagery Meditations in that they also work with images. The difference is that these images are metaphors for underlying emotional issues that lock inside our bodies and minds causing physical and psychological problems.

Release Meditations work best when you, consciously (before meditation) or subconsciously (during meditation), come up with an image that represents a negative emotion. Using a metaphoric image that represents a negative emotion is a powerful healing tool for two reasons.

First, ascribing an image to a problem, allows for commonality between your conscious and subconscious mind. Remember, our subconscious communicates best through images, symbols, metaphors, memories and emotions. Secondly, by reframing the negative emotion as a metaphoric image, the emotionality of the feeling becomes more neutral. This allows the emotion to be processed and released more easily.

When trying to come up with an image that can be seen, heard, smelled, or sensed consider how the emotion feels in your body or mind.

Let's take an example of uncontrolled anger. How does it feel in the body? Tense muscles. How does it feel in the mind? Racing thoughts. **Now consider those feelings and give them an image.** Perhaps tense muscles can be seen as a tight rubber band around your chest and racing thoughts as jagged lightning.

Working with a metaphoric image (rubber band around your chest) is preferred over processing a feeling (tense muscles). Using a metaphor places the emotion a distance away, where it can be processed and released more readily than getting hooked back into the drama of it all.

Only one image is needed as the focus, and it doesn't matter if it's an image that was drawn from a feeling in the body or mind. You only need one loose thread to unravel and free negative emotions.

When practicing a Release Meditation, you may think of the image ahead of time or after you are calm and relaxed. Sometimes when you're in a meditative state, a totally different image may appear. Whichever image you choose, acknowledge it and ask for understanding.

Once the image is clear, the next step is to process it. To process an image, follow these prompts:

- **Observe the image closely.**
- **Tell it how you feel.**
- **Have it respond.**
- **Ask the image what it wants from you.**
- **Have it respond.**
- **Tell the image what you want.**
- **Have it respond.**

Further dialogue can be added, until there is resolution or change.

Change occurs in many ways. The image may change color, size, texture, its placement to your body. This shows that something is happening. When the image becomes less intrusive, softer, not as threatening, some healing is occurring. Should the image suddenly flip and become a healing image, this indicates the negative emotion has been released. Sometimes the image is stubborn and won't answer back. If you've run out of questions, accept this.

When I first learned about this process I was skeptical. Talking to images in your head? How crazy is that? But it works. And it especially works when the images talk back!

Release meditations can be emotional. Know that where there is emotion there is truth. When possible, stay on the edge of the emotion until it passes. If the emotion is too difficult to handle, bring forth healing light, or any other resource available to you, i.e., totem animal (Totem Animal Meditation #25), wise one (Wise One Meditation #84), saint (Saint Meditation #100.) If the feeling remains overwhelming, allow it to be and gently awake.

When doing Release Meditations, journaling is important. Often times, change occurs but more work needs to be done. Document what happened and how you will proceed the next time. It's not unusual to bring forth that same image or a different image to do more clearing.

In the Release Meditations below, I've also included alternative meditations. These can be used if you can't come up with a metaphoric image or if you want to try a different approach. As with other meditations, begin with a favorite Processing Meditation that settles your body and mind.

**Meditation Basics:**
- **Put aside twenty minutes.**
- **Set a receptive tone.**
- **Relax your body.**
- **Clear your mind.**
- **Focus.**
- **Give gratitude.**
- **Journal.**

56. **Anger Release Meditation** – Relax and breathe deeply. When your mind is clear, think of an image that represents anger. It can be an image of how it feels in your body or mind. When the image is clear, process it by following the prompts on page 48. Alternate Meditation: Imagine a red ball of fire. How far is it from you? What's feeding it? How is it affecting you? Observe every detail. When ready, decide how best to deal with it. **Focus: Anger image or ball of fire.**

57. **Jealousy Release Meditation** – Relax and breathe deeply. When your mind is clear, think of an image that represents jealousy. It can be an image of how it feels in your body or mind. When the image is clear, process it by following the prompts on page 48. Alternate Meditation: Imagine a blackboard in front of you. Write down words that express how jealousy feels. Once finished, take an eraser and wipe them off the

board. With a blank board in front of you, write down words describing how you feel now that you have a clean slate. **Focus: Jealousy image or words on a blackboard.**

58. **Anxiety Release Meditation** – Relax and breathe deeply. When your mind is clear, think of an image that represents anxiety. It can be an image of how it feels in your body or mind. When the image is clear, process it by following the prompts on page 48. Alternate Meditation: Bring to mind an anxious state, what is happening and how you are feeling. In the background, either behind or to the side, think of an experience that is calming, safe and enjoyable. When ready, return to the anxious state, then flip the two images, where the anxious state falls into the background and the safe, comfortable experience leaps into the foreground. Do this until the positive experience and feelings fill the entire foreground and the anxious state can no longer be imagined. **Focus: Anxiety image or image flip.**

59. **Weight Release Meditation** – Weight issues result from a combination of many emotions and there are a number of ways to address them utilizing meditation. You could recall a specific memory (Pivotal Memory Meditation #54) of when you first had weight issues and look at it from different perspectives. You could bring forth your inner child (Inner Child Meditation #55) and discuss the matter. You could process one image then work on another. Example: Weight could

feel like a ball and chain one day, but a spare tire around your waist the next day. Relax and breathe deeply. When your mind is clear, think of an image that represents weight. It can be an image of how it feels in your body or mind. When the image is clear, process it by following the prompts on page 48. Alternate Meditation: Imagine yourself at an ideal weight. How does this make you feel? How do you look? What activities do you participate in? Experience this ideal weight in detail. **Focus: Weight image or ideal weight image.**

60. **Smoking Release Meditation** – Relax and breathe deeply. When your mind is clear, think of an image that represents smoking. It can be an image of how it feels in your body or mind. When the image is clear, process it by following the prompts on page 48. Alternate Meditation: Imagine a smoke-free day in your life from the moment you awake until you fall back to sleep. Watch yourself. How do you feel, look, act? Then imagine parts of your body: mouth, sinuses, throat, lungs, heart. How does the clean, clear air affect these body parts? **Focus: Smoking image or a smoke-free day.**

61. **Guilt Release Meditation** – Relax and breathe deeply. When your mind is clear, think of an image that represents guilt. It can be an image of how it feels in your body or mind. When the image is clear, process it by following the prompts on page 48. Alternate Meditation: Imagine going into your closet, opening the door,

and finding an item that no longer suits you. Pull it out and observe it carefully. Why do you keep it? What purpose does it serve? Decide how you want to proceed and act on this decision. Evaluate and remove as many items as you like. **Focus: Guilt image or clothes in closet.**

62. **Depression Release Meditation** – Relax and breathe deeply. When your mind is clear, think of an image that represents depression. It can be an image of how it feels in your body or mind. When the image is clear, process it by following the prompts on page 48. Alternate Meditation: Imagine a healing place that is safe and draws you in. It could be your special place or a different place. Take a few moments and experience this healing place in detail, i.e., temperature, light, colors. Breathe deeply and enjoy this spot, knowing it is a healing place. Absorb its calming energy, a soothing balm to your spirit. Should emotions come up, release them. **Focus: Depression image or special healing place.**

63. **Worry Release Meditation** – Relax and breathe deeply. When your mind is clear, think of an image that represents worry. It can be an image of how it feels in your body or mind. When the image is clear, process it by following the prompts on page 48. Alternate Meditation: In your mind, write one worry on a slip of paper, crumple it up and toss it onto the floor. Proceed identifying every worry. After each worry is written down, crumpled and tossed, look at the

floor. What would you like to do next? In your mind's eye, act on your decision. **Focus: Worry image or crumpled paper.**

64. **Habit Release Meditation** – Relax and breathe deeply. When your mind is clear, think of an image that represents a habit you'd like to break. It can be an image of how this habit feels in your body or mind. When the image is clear, process it by following the prompts on page 48. Alternate Meditation: In your mind imagine what it would be like to be free of this habit. Watch yourself carefully as you go through the day. How do you not succumb to the habit? Experience and enjoy the freedom of your choices. **Focus: Habit image or a day without the habit.**

65. **Grief Release Meditation** – Grief is a complicated emotion that involves guilt, sadness, blame, and loss. Therefore to process an image of grief, consider any one of the above emotions. Relax and breathe deeply. When your mind is clear, think of an image that represents grief. It can be an image of how it feels in your body or mind. When the image is clear, process it by following the prompts on page 48. Alternate Meditation: Imagine a healing white energy traveling into your body. Have it pass to parts that feel gray or thick or cold. Feel this energy as it soothes and calms. If any emotions surface, allow them to rise up and away from your body. When cleared, replace the emptiness with the love you've felt for a special person, pet or place. **Focus: Grief image or healing energy.**

Release Meditations

66. **Loneliness Release Meditation** – Relax and breathe deeply. When your mind is clear, think of an image that represents loneliness. It can be an image of how it feels in your body or mind. When the image is clear, process it by following the prompts on page 48. Alternate Meditation: Loneliness is a feeling of unconnected-ness and isolation to others and to ourselves. When relaxed and your mind is clear, visit your special place. What person, place or thing draws your interest? Approach it, introduce yourself, and tell it how you feel. Allow it to respond. **Focus: Loneliness image or special place dialogue.**

67. **Frustration Release Meditation** – Relax and breathe deeply. When your mind is clear, think of an image that represents frustration. It can be an image of how it feels in your body or mind. When the image is clear, process it by following the prompts on page 48. Alternate Meditation: Think of a recent moment when you were frustrated. When ready, recall this moment but instead of reacting, step to the side to avoid its onslaught. Watch in detachment as the frustrating moment misses you and travels off into the distance. **Focus: Frustration image or a moment of frustration.**

68. **Fear Release Meditation** – Relax and breathe deeply. When your mind is clear, think of an image that represents a fear that you have. It can be an image of how it feels in your body or mind. When the image is clear, process it by following the prompts on page 48. Alternate

Meditation: Imagine sitting at a desk in familiar surroundings and welcoming your fear to sit opposite you. Observe the fear carefully, calmly, knowing you are safe and in control. How does this fear look to you? Interview this fear. Ask it any question and allow it to answer. When finished with the interview, breathe easily and effortlessly. **Focus: Fear image or interview with fear.**

69. **Pain Release Meditation** – Before proceeding, understand that pain is your body signaling an SOS. When in pain, first seek medical advice. Once diagnosed, utilize this meditation as an adjunct to treatment. Relax and breathe deeply. When your mind is clear, think of an image that represents pain. It can be an image of how it feels in your body or mind. When the image is clear, process it by following the prompts on page 48. Alternate Meditation: Imagine your pain is a tunnel that you can enter. At the threshold, the pain is great. Once inside a light shines at the far end. With each step you take, the pain lessens. Proceed as the light grows stronger. Follow the light until you exit the tunnel. **Focus: Pain image or light tunnel.**

70. **Panic Release Meditation** – Relax and breathe deeply. When your mind is clear, think of an image that represents a panic attack. It can be an image of how it feels in your body or mind. When the image is clear, process it by following the prompts on page 48. Alternate Meditation: Imagine yourself sitting in a theater. The movie

you are about to watch is a replay of a panic attack. Get comfortable knowing you are safe and in control. When ready, watch the film of yourself on the screen. Should you become uncomfortable, fast forward the action. When the movie is over, rewind it backwards at a fast pace, and replay. When you are able to watch the film with no panic response, decide what you want to do to the film. **Focus: Panic image or past panic attack review.**

71. **Stress Release Meditation** – Relax and breathe deeply. When your mind is clear, think of an image that represents stress. It can be an image of how it feels in your body or mind. When the image is clear, process it by following the prompts on page 48. Alternate Meditation: Imagine yourself at work or at home where there is a great deal of stress and pressure. Observe yourself carefully. When ready imagine a shield descending around you. It can be any color, any style. Allow this shield to encapsulate you. Observe how the stressors bounce off the shield away from you. You are safe and for each moment you remain inside this shield you are protected and can breathe easily. **Focus: Stress image or protective shield.**

72. **Burden Release Meditation** – Relax and breathe deeply. When your mind is clear, think of a burden you are carrying. It can be an image of how it feels in your body or mind. When the image is clear, process it by following the prompts on page 48. Alternate Meditation:

Imagine you are climbing a steep hill. In your backpack are rocks of different sizes and colors. When you are tired and unable to move forward, look inside your pack and pull out one of the stones. What burden is written on the stone? When ready, cast it off. Continue climbing and divesting yourself of the weights you are carrying. Enjoy the vista from atop the hill. **Focus: Burden image or climbing a hill.**

73. **Obstacle Release Meditation** – Relax and breathe deeply. When your mind is clear, think of an image that represents an obstacle. It can be an image of how it feels in your body or mind. When the image is clear, process it by following the prompts on page 48. Alternate meditation: Return to your special place. Look around and sense if you notice an obstruction of any kind (i.e. fallen branch.) Approach the spot and observe this obstacle carefully. When ready, free yourself from this problem in any manner. If it's too large or cumbersome, begin a conversation by telling it how you feel. **Focus: Obstacle image or blockage in special place.**

74. **Negativity Release Meditation** – Relax and breathe deeply. When your mind is clear, think of an image that represents negativity. It can be an image of how it feels in your body or mind. When the image is clear, process it by following the prompts on page 48. Alternate meditation: Observe from a detached viewpoint thoughts or feelings that come into your mind. Should any thought or emotion appear negative, give it no

value, and let it leave your mind in any manner you feel is appropriate, i.e., showing it the door. To help with this meditation, bring forth a wise one (Wise One Meditation #84). Sit together and evaluate thoughts and feelings for their negative nature. When determined, allow such thoughts or feelings to leave. **Focus: Negativity image or thought evaluation.**

The following Release Meditations address physical manifestations of stress and disease. **Please note that meditation does not take the place of medical intervention but is a holistic aid to facilitate the healing process.**

75. **Allergy Release Meditation** – Relax and breathe deeply. When your mind is clear, think of an image that represents how an allergy makes you feel. It can be an image of how it feels in your body or mind. When the image is clear, process it by following the prompts on page 48. Alternate meditation: When relaxed and calm, imagine that you are symptom free. Experience every aspect of not having this allergy in vivid detail. **Focus: Allergy image or allergy free image.**

76. **Asthma Release Meditation** – Relax and breathe deeply. When your mind is clear, think of an image that represents how having an asthma attack feels. It can be an image of how it feels in your body or mind. When the image is clear, process it by following the prompts on page 48. Alternate Meditation: When relaxed and calm,

imagine a place where you can breathe freely and effortlessly. Imagine the comfort and confidence in knowing you are safe, in control, and healthy. Allow your lungs to open and breathe easily. Experience how the oxygenated air passes into your lungs and finds a welcoming, receptive organ. **Focus: Asthma image or easy breath session.**

77. **Cancer Release Meditation** – Relax and breathe deeply. When your mind is clear, think of an image that represents how having cancer feels. It can be an image of how it feels in your body or mind. When the image is clear, process it by following the prompts on page 48. Alternate Meditation: Imagine cancer cells as weak, small, few in number, vague in coloration when a strong, colorful, active, powerful interloper comes to get rid of them. **Focus: Cancer image or helpful interloper.**

78. **Headache Release Meditation** – Relax and breathe deeply. When your mind is clear, think of an image that represents how having a headache feels. It can be an image of how it feels in your body or mind. When the image is clear, process it by following the prompts on page 48. Alternate Meditation: Imagine the many muscles located throughout your head, neck and shoulders. Begin in one spot and slowly loosen the muscles located around the circumference of your head (forehead, above ears, around the hairline), then loosen the muscles in your face (around eyes, sinuses, cheeks, jaw), followed by the muscles

located in the back of your neck. Finally, relax the muscles that travel down your shoulders. To help relax these muscles, stretch or contract them first. **Focus: Headache image or progressive relaxation of muscles.**

79. **High Blood Pressure Release Meditation** – Relax and breathe deeply. When your mind is clear, think of an image that represents how having high blood pressure feels. It can be an image of how it feels in your body or mind. When the image is clear, process it by following the prompts on page 48. Alternate Meditation: (Before beginning, consider taking your blood pressure.) Recall an activity you enjoyed as a child. Take yourself back to those moments and relive in detail. Experience these moments as if you are actually doing them. Enjoy this activity for the entire session. (When finished, retake blood pressure.) **Focus: Blood pressure image or enjoyable memory.**

80. **Irritable Bowel Release Meditation** – Relax and breathe deeply. When your mind is clear, think of an image that represents how having an IBS attack feels. It can be an image of how it feels in your body or mind. When the image is clear, process it by following the prompts on page 48. Alternate Meditation: Imagine your lower abdomen when it is in distress. Look inside and note the color, size, and what's happening. Breathe to that part of the body and watch the image change. **Focus: IBS image or visualization of abdomen.**

81. **Tension Release Meditation** – Relax and breathe deeply. When your mind is clear, think of an image that represents how tension feels. It can be an image of how it feels in your body or mind. When the image is clear, process it by following the prompts on page 48. Alternate Meditation: Imagine taking inventory of your inner body. Observe and sense the muscles from your head down to your toes. Do a slow scan evaluating any tight areas. When found, breathe into them, loosening them and allowing the stiffness to soften. Move throughout your body, until every area is loose, warm and soft. **Focus: Tension image or muscle scan.**

82. **Viral Infection Release Meditation** – Relax and breathe deeply. When your mind is clear, think of an image that represents how having a cold or flu feels. It can be an image of how it feels in your body or mind. When the image is clear, process it by following the prompts on page 48. Alternate Meditation: Imagine a thick liquid inside your body. Give it a color, texture (whatever you choose), and watch it carefully. When ready, draw in a healing color (whatever you choose), and have it react with the cold or flu image. As the image changes, allow it to dissipate from your body in whatever manner is appropriate. **Focus: Viral infection image or healing color.**

83. **Condition Release Meditation** – For any unspecified health condition, follow the same instructions. Relax and breathe deeply. When

your mind is clear, think of an image that represents how this condition feels. It can be an image of how it feels in your body or mind. When the image is clear, process it by following the prompts on page 48. Alternate Meditation: In your mind's eye, visit the source of this condition. Observe this image carefully. What is needed to restore this area to full vibrant health? Use all the tools available to you: your wise one (Wise One Meditation #84), totem animal (Totem Animal Meditation #25), healing light (Healing Light Meditation #87). **Focus: Any health concern image or active understanding to restore health.**

## Inspirational Meditations

Inspirational Meditations combine imagery with the divine, our higher selves, nature, and/or positive thought. Similar to Processing Meditations, these meditations are global in scope and can be used as a component in other types of meditation. Example: A wise one, once established, can be used as an advisor when doing a Release Meditation. Inspirational Meditations have, at their core, powerful healing and transpersonal properties that are accessible and enjoyable.

**Meditation Basics:**
- **Put aside twenty minutes.**
- **Set a receptive tone.**
- **Relax your body.**
- **Clear your mind.**
- **Focus.**
- **Give gratitude.**
- **Journal.**

84. **Wise One Meditation** – This meditation helps to discover a wise one who can help you during

meditative practice or regular waking moments. The wise one supports you, gives advice, and/or can be a guide. The wise one can take endless forms, i.e., angel, totem animal, your higher self, God, a color, a thing. There are many ways to discover a wise one. It could be located in your special place or crop up as an image in another meditation. A wise one may originally appear undefined and vague (a color, a sound, a taste, a word.) Whenever an image reappears or remains constant, take the time to ask it a question. If the answer is surprising, hopeful, insightful, this may be your wise one. Another way to discover a wise one is to thank your wise one for all the good decisions (be specific) you've made in your life. When finished, ask the wise one to come forward with a message. Listen or be alert to whatever comes. Develop interaction by asking questions and dialoguing. **Focus: Discovering a wise one.**

85. **Gratitude Meditation** – Gratitude is powerful because it honors the gifts received. And honoring gifts encourages the loving energy, abundant universe, to give more. Once relaxed in body and clear in mind, select one gift to be thankful for. Sense this gift in its many facets and give gratitude to each aspect. When finished, observe in all ways possible this gift's response to your gratitude. **Focus: Giving gratitude.**

86. **Forgiveness Meditation** – Like gratitude, forgiveness is a powerful act that frees. When

relaxed and calm, fill your body with loving, forgiving energy, however you define it. This energy can come in on a breath or in a color of your choosing. When you feel forgiveness think of someone who needs forgiving and send that energy to him or her. Once completed, think of those who you've made suffer, and ask for their forgiveness. The final forgiveness is for yourself. **Focus: Forgiveness.**

87. **Healing Light Meditation** – Breathe, relax, clear your mind. When you are ready, imagine a rainbow. See it, feel it, or experience it in whatever way you like. When ready, take one color from the rainbow and draw it closer to you. Allow this healing light to wash over and through you, healing and cleansing every nerve, muscle, organ, bone of your body. For the duration of the meditation follow it as it travels the pathways of the body. Color can change during session or for other sessions. **Focus: Healing light.**

88. **Healing Hand Meditation** – Breathe, relax, clear your mind. When ready, open one hand and draw energy to it. This can be done by sending your breath to the hand or having light energy warm it. Concentrate on the healing nature of your hand as it warms. Kindly place your hand on any part of your body that needs healing energy. **Focus: Healing hand.**

89. **Empowerment Meditation** – After relaxing your body and quieting your thoughts, imagine climbing a steep mountain. The peak is near and

you are breathing heavily. Experience the moment when you come to the peak. Once atop the mountain, note the vista, the temperature, the light. Enjoy the many aspects in detail. Then slowly pan away, watching yourself atop a mountain, solid, assured, and ready to receive gifts from the universe. **Focus: Power from the universe.**

90. **Peace Meditation** – When body is relaxed and mind is clear, feel the peace and restfulness in your body. When ready, think of someone you love and feel this sensation around your heart. Imagine a way to project this feeling outward to those who are not at peace. Where there is strife and suffering, envision a white light coming down healing wounds, broken hearts, and fears. Finally, project a hopeful image, i.e., doves, to areas of the world that need healing. **Focus: Sending out peace.**

91. **Feed the Soul Meditation** – When relaxed in body and mind, imagine a banquet in front of you. This banquet is in honor of your spirit. Bring your spirit to the bountiful table. In your mind's eye, imagine the event in vivid detail. Whatever your spirit wants, needs or likes, have it available. **Focus: Spirit celebration.**

92. **Insight Meditation** – When relaxed and mind is clear, think of a devastating event in your life. Consider this moment, then ask the question: What was good about this event? Answer, then ask what was good about the answer you just

gave. Proceed asking and answering questions until you arrive at a final answer of peace, love or oneness. Yes. All answers lead to this place. Example: Got in a car crash. What was good about this? Answer: Didn't have to go to work. What was good about this? Answer: Could stay home and watch TV. What was good about this? Answer: Didn't have to worry. What was good about this? Answer: I felt calmer. What was good about this? Answer: Could appreciate my family more. What was good about this? Answer: I'm loved. **Focus: Event reframe.**

93. **Manifestation Meditation** – Relax your body and clear your mind. When ready imagine a place and time in the future. Look around and observe every detail. Observe yourself in these surroundings: how you look, what you're doing, the way you feel. **Focus: Event in future.**

94. **Witness Meditation** – Relax, breathe and clear your mind. When ready, be a witness to sensory details, emotions, thoughts, and impressions that float through your mind. With each detail noticed, acknowledge it, then release it, knowing it is temporary. When distanced from these impressions, merge with your conscious witness. **Focus: Detached observer.**

95. **Creativity Meditation** – Relax, breathe and clear your mind. When ready, design a creative space filled with all the tools needed to complete your creative endeavor. Get comfortable there and explore. Like a special place, this meditation

can be revisited anytime, including when you have a blockage. When stuck, find what may be causing problems in this space, then process it by telling it how you feel and what you want to have happen. **Focus: Increase creativity.**

96. **Back at cha Meditation** – This is a waking meditation to exchange energy between yourself and an object. The object can be anything – a flower, a stone, even yourself in the mirror. When you are relaxed and your mind is clear, simply look at the object. As you concentrate on it, what energy emanates from it? What are the different ways this object can be experienced. Besides seeing it, can it be smelled, heard, felt? Ponder the object further. What energy can you send to it? With concentration, an emotion may surface; blurred boundaries between yourself and the object may arise; a sense of oneness may be felt. **Focus: Energy exchange.**

97. **Elements Meditation** – Breathe to relax and calm the mind. When ready, think of the four elements: earth, water, air, fire. Experience or visualized one element at a time, first in nature, then inside your body. Example: water in a river, blood in an artery. Once you carefully contemplate the four elements both in nature and in your body, extend yourself to oneness with nature. **Focus: Merging of nature with body.**

98. **Pink Bubble Meditation** – This meditation is based on the laws of attraction. Breathe and relax your body. With a clear uncluttered mind,

imagine a desire or dream you want to come true. Imagine this desire or dream as coming true. Experience this desire or dream in fine detail. Now place this desire or dream inside a pink bubble and release it into the universe, where it can gather energy and come back as a manifestation. **Focus: Dream manifestation.**

99. **Savior Meditation** – Relax your body and mind. When ready, imagine kneeling in front of your Savior. Imagine this scene with great detail. What are your thoughts? How do you feel? When ready, make an offering. It can be anything you wish: suffering, pain, gratitude. How is your offering accepted? **Focus: Interaction with Savior.**

100. **Saint Meditation** – Relax your body and mind. When ready, visualize a saint or spiritual icon standing in front of you. To make the image more vivid, look at his/her feet. Visualize each detail as your eyes rise up his/her body. What is he/she wearing? Follow to his/her face. How does he/she react to you. Engage in conversation. **Focus: Conversation with saint.**

101. **Omniprescence Meditation** – Relax your body and mind. When ready, experience in any manner you choose, a person, a place, a thing, a memory that encompasses love in the form of peace, tranquility, connected-ness. As you contemplate this form of love, allow it to build and extend beyond your physical body to merge with the universe, where every minute particle to

the grandness of space is filled with unity and oneness. **Focus: Connection with God, higher power, love, or energy.**

## Author's Note...

Several years ago, I was the Senior Clinician at the VISA program, a ten-day student intervention program, run by the Buffalo Board of Education and the University at Buffalo. Working with two facilitators and several grad-student interns, it was our job to provide group counseling for two periods during the academic day for students suspended for violence, usually inner-city males between the ages of 13 to 17.

Since no canned program existed to fit our time constraints, I put together a curriculum from other life skill programs that addressed conflict resolution, anger management, stress reduction, self-esteem, among others.

We also implemented team building activities and anything else that seemed to get their attention. And there was one special something that did get their attention. It happened on the day allocated for stress reduction – a ten-minute guided meditation of being on a beach.

I was shocked at how easily the students closed their eyes and remained quiet. Unfortunately, it was years later after I was trained in holistic therapies, that I understood how we had stumbled upon, but failed to realize, a powerful, simple modality that could have been expanded to make true change, change that happens from within.

But it's never too late. While tossing a grenade into water isn't fishing, dropping a hook and a line is.

Best of luck.

## Suggestions...

- There are many wonderful books on self-help, meditation, healing imagery, transpersonal therapy but my favorite is *The Amazing Power of Deliberate Intent: Living the Art of Allowing* by Esther and Jerry Hicks.

- Music CDs abound. The one I've worn thin is *Relaxation and Meditation with Music and Nature: Summer Solitude.* Laserlight Series.

- To further your meditative practice, start or join a meditation circle that meets regularly. Activities can include: a group meditation, sharing of meditations, insights gained, new meditations discovered.

- To jumpstart your meditative practice, a 31-day journal follows. Included are prompts (if you choose to use them), inspirational quotes, and blank space for drawings and doodles. A journal documents progress and maps out ideas for future sessions – all grist for the self-discovery mill.

# meditation journal

Your crossing awaits...

101 Ways to Meditate

**Checklist:**
___ 20 minutes   ___ Receptive Tone   ___ Gratitude

## Drawings and Doodles

Meditation Journal

## **Day One**

*It does not matter how slowly you go so long as you do not stop.* – Confucius

Relaxation Meditation (#1)

Notes:
_____

_____
_____
_____
_____
_____
_____
_____
_____
_____
_____
_____
_____
_____
_____

Ideas for future session:

_____
_____
_____

**Checklist:**
___ 20 minutes  ___ Receptive Tone  ___ Gratitude

## Drawings and Doodles

Meditation Journal

## **Day Two**

*This is your world, I'm just livin' in it.*
– Banks, Homer; Crutcher, Betty; Parker, William Dean

Special Place Meditation (#22)

Notes:
_____
_____
_____
_____
_____
_____
_____
_____
_____
_____
_____
_____
_____
_____
_____
_____

Ideas for future session:
_____
_____
_____

**Checklist:**
___ 20 minutes   ___ Receptive Tone   ___ Gratitude

## Drawings and Doodles

## Day Three

*Think of all the beauty still around you and be happy.* – Anne Frank

Elements Meditation (#97)

Notes:
_____
_____
_____
_____
_____
_____
_____
_____
_____
_____
_____
_____
_____
_____
_____
_____

Ideas for future session:
_____
_____
_____

**Checklist:**
  ___ 20 minutes    ___ Receptive Tone    ___ Gratitude

## Drawings and Doodles

Meditation Journal

## Day Four

*Let each man exercise the art he knows.*
-Aristophanes

Inner Sound Meditation (#14)

Notes:

Ideas for future session:

**Checklist:**
　　___ 20 minutes　　___ Receptive Tone　　___ Gratitude

## Drawings and Doodles

Meditation Journal

## **Day Five**

*The cure for boredom is curiosity. There is no cure for curiosity.* – Dorothy Parker

Wise One Meditation (#84)

Notes:
_____
_____
_____
_____
_____
_____
_____
_____
_____
_____
_____
_____
_____
_____
_____

Ideas for future session:
_____
_____
_____
_____

101 Ways to Meditate

**Checklist:**
    __ 20 minutes    __ Receptive Tone    __ Gratitude

## Drawing and Doodles

## Day Six

*Order is not pressure which is imposed on society from without, but an equilibrium that is set from within.*
– José Ortega y Gasset

Anger Release Meditation (#56)

Notes:

Ideas for future session:

**Checklist:**
___ 20 minutes   ___ Receptive Tone   ___ Gratitude

## Drawings and Doodles

Meditation Journal

## **Day Seven**

*Occupy your destiny.*
– Peter L. Kirsch

Manifestation Meditation (#93)

Notes:

Ideas for future session:

**Checklist:**
    \_\_ 20 minutes     \_\_ Receptive Tone     \_\_ Gratitude

## Drawings and Doodles

## Day Eight

*If we did all the things we are capable of, we would astound ourselves.* – Thomas Edison

Creativity Meditation (#95)

Notes:

Ideas for future session:

101 Ways to Meditate

**Checklist:**
___ 20 minutes   ___ Receptive Tone   ___ Gratitude

## **Drawings and Doodles**

## Day Nine

*Fear less, hope more, eat less, chew more, whine less, breathe more, talk less, say more, hate less, love more, and good things will be yours.* – Swedish Proverb

Loving Kindness Meditation (#12)

Notes:

Ideas for future session:

101 Ways to Meditate

**Checklist:**
    ___ 20 minutes     ___ Receptive Tone     ___ Gratitude

## Drawings and Doodles

Meditation Journal

## **Day Ten**

*Not knowing when the dawn will come,
I open every door.*– Emily Dickinson

Drop of Rain Meditation (#27)

Notes:

Ideas for future session:

101 Ways to Meditate

**Checklist:**
___ 20 minutes   ___ Receptive Tone   ___ Gratitude

## Drawings and Doodles

## Day Eleven

Our lack of compassion stems from our inability to see deeply into the nature of things. – Lama Surya Das

Insight Meditation (#92)

Notes:

Ideas for future session:

**Checklist:**
    \_\_ 20 minutes     \_\_ Receptive Tone     \_\_ Gratitude

## Drawings and Doodles

## Day Twelve

The most beautiful things in the world are not seen nor touched. They are felt with the heart. – Helen Keller

Kindness Meditation (#37)

Notes:

Ideas for future session:

101 Ways to Meditate

**Checklist:**
　　__ 20 minutes　　__ Receptive Tone　　__ Gratitude

## **Drawings and Doodles**

## Day Thirteen

*A bird doesn't sing because it has an answer, it sings because it has a song.* – Maya Angelou

Gratitude Meditation (#85)

Notes:

Ideas for future session:

**Checklist:**
  ___ 20 minutes   ___ Receptive Tone   ___ Gratitude

## Drawings and Doodles

## Day Fourteen

*In every out-thrust headland, in every curving beach, in every grain of sand, there is the story of the earth.*
– Rachel Carson

Back at Cha Meditation (#96)

Notes:

Ideas for future session:

**Checklist:**
  __ 20 minutes   __ Receptive Tone   __ Gratitude

## Drawings and Doodles

## Day Fifteen

*People are not lazy. They simply have impotent goals - that is, goals that do not inspire them.* – Tony Robbins

Success Meditation (#38)

Notes:

Ideas for future session:

**Checklist:**
    \_\_ 20 minutes     \_\_ Receptive Tone     \_\_ Gratitude

## Drawings and Doodles

## Day Sixteen

*Always laugh when you can. It's cheap medicine.*
*– Lord Byron*

Laughing Buddha Meditation (#20)

Notes:
_____
_____
_____
_____
_____
_____
_____
_____
_____
_____
_____
_____
_____
_____
_____
_____

Ideas for future session:
_____
_____
_____

**Checklist:**
　　___ 20 minutes　　___ Receptive Tone　　___ Gratitude

## Drawings and Doodles

Meditation Journal

## Day Seventeen

*Don't kill the dream - execute it.*
– Unknown

Spontaneous Image Meditation (#34)

Notes:

Ideas for future session:

101 Ways to Meditate

**Checklist:**
  __ 20 minutes      __ Receptive Tone      __ Gratitude

## Drawings and Doodles

Meditation Journal

## **Day Eighteen**

*Life shrinks or expands in proportion to one's courage.*
— Anais Nin

Panic Release Meditation (#70)

Notes:

Ideas for future session:

## 101 Ways to Meditate

**Checklist:**
　　__ 20 minutes　　__ Receptive Tone　　__ Gratitude

# Drawings and Doodles

## Day Nineteen

*Genuine poetry can communicate before it is understood.* – T.S. Eliot

Pink Bubble Meditation (#98)

Notes:

Ideas for future session:

## 101 Ways to Meditate

**Checklist:**
　　__ 20 minutes　　__ Receptive Tone　　__ Gratitude

# Drawings and Doodles

## Day Twenty

*Live Yes.* – Linda A. Lavid

Negativity Release Meditation (#74)

Notes:

Ideas for future session:

**Checklist**:
___ 20 minutes   ___ Receptive Tone   ___ Gratitude

## Drawings and Doodles

## Day Twenty-One

*The violets in the mountains have broken the rocks.*
– Tennessee Williams

Empowerment Meditation (#89)

Notes:

Ideas for future session:

## 101 Ways to Meditate

**Checklist:**
___ 20 minutes     ___ Receptive Tone     ___ Gratitude

# Drawings and Doodles

## Day Twenty-Two

*Never think you've seen the last of anything.*
– Eudora Welty

Details of a Special Place Meditation (#23)

Notes:

Ideas for future session:

**Checklist:**
　　___ 20 minutes　　___ Receptive Tone　　___ Gratitude

## Drawings and Doodles

## Day Twenty-Three

*In the faces of men and women I see God.*
  – Walt Whitman

Omnipresence Meditation (#101)

Notes:

Ideas for future session:

101 Ways to Meditate

**Checklist:**
　　 __ 20 minutes　　 __ Receptive Tone　　 __ Gratitude

## Drawings and Doodles

## Day Twenty-Four

*What I dream of is an art of balance, of purity and serenity devoid of troubling or depressing subject matter.* – Henri Matisse

Totem Animal Meditation (#25)

Notes:

Ideas for future session:

101 Ways to Meditate

**Checklist:**
___ 20 minutes   ___ Receptive Tone   ___ Gratitude

## **Drawings and Doodles**

## Day Twenty-Five

*When you dance alone, spirit is your partner.*
– Linda A. Lavid

Movement Meditation (#19)

Notes:

Ideas for future session:

**Checklist:**
    \_\_ 20 minutes    \_\_ Receptive Tone    \_\_ Gratitude

## Drawings and Doodles

## **Day Twenty-Six**

*Faith is taking the first step even when you don't see the whole staircase.* – Martin Luther King, Jr.

Fear Release Meditation (#68)

Notes:

Ideas for future session:

**Checklist:**
　　__ 20 minutes　　__ Receptive Tone　　__ Gratitude

# Drawings and Doodles

## Day Twenty-Seven

*Breathe. Let go. And remind yourself that this very moment is the only one you know you have for sure.*
– Oprah Winfrey

Breath Meditation (#2)

Notes:

Ideas for future session:

**Checklist:**
   __ 20 minutes    __ Receptive Tone    __ Gratitude

## Drawings and Doodles

## Day Twenty-Eight

*When I let go of what I am, I become what I might be.*
  – Lao Tzu

Obstacle Release Meditation (#73)

Notes:

Ideas for future session:

101 Ways to Meditate

**Checklist:**
    \_\_ 20 minutes     \_\_ Receptive Tone     \_\_ Gratitude

# Drawings and Doodles

Meditation Journal

## **Day Twenty-Nine**

*Your imagination is your preview of life's coming attractions.* – Albert Einstein

Seed Planting Meditation (#31)

Notes:

Ideas for future session:

101 Ways to Meditate

**Checklist:**
___ 20 minutes   ___ Receptive Tone   ___ Gratitude

# Drawings and Doodles

## **Day Thirty**

*Again a different meaning has to be understood.*
— Buddha

Inner Child Meditation (#55)

Notes:

Ideas for future session:

**Checklist:**
　　__ 20 minutes　　__ Receptive Tone　　__ Gratitude

# Drawings and Doodles

## Day Thirty-One

*With the catching ends the pleasure of the chase.*
– Abraham Lincoln

Question Meditation (#32)

Notes:

Ideas for future session:

## Index of Meditation

**4-4-8 Meditation** ......................................... 25

**Adjustment Meditation** ............................... 41

**Allergy Release Meditation** ......................... 59

**Anger Release Meditation** .......................... 50

**Anxiety Release Meditation** ....................... 51

**Asthma Release Meditation** ....................... 60

**Back at cha Meditation** .............................. 70

**Body Celebration Meditation** ...................... 39

**Body Scan Meditation** ................................ 27

**Breath Meditation** ..................................... 25

**Burden Release Meditation** ........................ 58

**Cancer Release Meditation** ........................ 60

**Chakra Meditation** .................................... 30

**Childbirth Meditation** ............................................. 42

**Condition Release Meditation** ....................... 63

**Creativity Meditation** ...................................... 69

**Departed One Meditation** ........................... 42

**Depression Release Meditation** ................... 53

**Details from a Special Place Meditation** ....... 34

**Draw Breath to Parts of the Body Meditation** ............................................................................... 27

**Drop of Rain Meditation** ............................. 36

**Elements Meditation** ...................................... 70

**Emotional Body Meditation** ......................... 43

**Empowerment Meditation** ........................... 67

**Enjoy a Bountiful Moment Meditation** .......... 35

**Favorite Memory Meditation** ....................... 45

**Fear Release Meditation** ............................... 56

**Feed the Soul Meditation** ............................ 68

**Forgiveness Meditation** ............................... 66

**Frustration Release Meditation** ................... 55

**Gift Meditation** ............................................. 36

**Gratitude Meditation** ................................. **66**

**Grief Release Meditation** ........................... **54**

**Grounding Meditation** ................................. **38**

**Guilt Release Meditation** ........................... **52**

**Habit Release Meditation** .......................... **54**

**Headache Release Meditation** .................... **61**

**Healing Hand Meditation** ........................... **67**

**Healing Light Meditation** ........................... **67**

**Healing Meditation** ..................................... **40**

**High Blood Pressure Release Meditation** ..... **61**

**Inner Child Meditation** ............................... **46**

**Inner Light/Screen Meditation** .................... **29**

**Inner Smile Meditation** ............................... **30**

**Inner Sound Meditation** ............................. **29**

**Insight Meditation** ...................................... **68**

**Integration Meditation** ............................... **44**

**Intellectual Body Meditation** ...................... **43**

**Irritable Bowel Release Meditation** ............. **62**

Jealousy Release Meditation ........................ 50

Kindness Meditation ..................................... 39

Kundalini Mantra Meditation ....................... 30

Laughing Buddha Meditation ....................... 31

Letting Go Meditation ................................... 40

Loneliness Release Meditation .................... 55

Loving Kindness (Metta) Meditation ............ 28

Manifestation Meditation ............................. 69

Mindful of the Moment (Mindfulness) Meditation ................................................. 25

Movement Meditation .................................. 31

Negativity Release Meditation ..................... 59

Not-Trying Meditation .................................. 29

Obstacle Release Meditation ....................... 58

Omniprescence Meditation .......................... 72

Open Doors Meditation ................................ 36

Pain Release Meditation .............................. 56

Panic Release Meditation ............................ 57

Peace Meditation .......................................... 68

**Performance Meditation** ............................ 38

**Pet Meditation** ........................................... 35

**Physical Body Meditation** ........................ 43

**Pink Bubble Meditation** ............................ 71

**Pivotal Memory Meditation** ...................... 45

**Plant Flowers Meditation** ......................... 37

**Post-Surgery Meditation** .......................... 42

**Prayer Meditation** ..................................... 26

**Pre-Surgery Meditation** ............................ 41

**Protector Meditation.** ................................ 41

**Question Meditation** ................................. 37

**Reduce Chatter Meditation** ...................... 28

**Relaxation Meditation** .............................. 24

**Saint Meditation** ....................................... 71

**Savior Meditation** ..................................... 71

**Simple Memory Meditation** ...................... 44

**Sit in Nature Meditation** ........................... 37

**Smoking Release Meditation** ................... 52

Special Place Meditation ............................. 34

Spiritual Body Meditation ............................ 44

Spontaneous Image Meditation ................... 38

Stress Release Meditation ........................... 57

Stretching Meditation .................................. 31

Success Meditation ...................................... 40

Taoist Meditation ......................................... 27

Tension Release Meditation ......................... 62

Totem Animal Meditation ............................ 35

Viral Infection Release Meditation .............. 62

Walking Meditation ...................................... 28

Weight Release Meditation .......................... 51

Wise One Meditation .................................... 65

Witness Meditation ...................................... 69

Word Repetition Meditation ........................ 26

Worry Release Meditation ........................... 53

**About the Author**

Award-winning author, Linda A. Lavid, holds a Master's degree in Social Work and is a certified hypnotherapist with a practice in healing imagery. For more information, visit: lindalavid.com

**Other Books by Linda A. Lavid:**

Rented Rooms: A Collection of Short Fiction

Paloma: A Laurent & Dove Mystery

Thirst: A Collection of Short Fiction

Composition: A Fiction Writer's Guide for the 21$^{st}$ Century

Weekly Strategies: Tips on Writing, Editing & more

On Creative Writing

Spots Blind: Stories

The Dying of Ed Mees: A Novella

Of the Dance/De la Danza: Bilingual Stories

The Simple Mechanic of Infinite Execution: A Novella

101 Maneras de Meditar: Descubra Su Verdadero Yo

Woman & Flight (art)

Mujer y Vuelo (arte)

Cats: Winsome & Wise (art)

Made in the USA
San Bernardino, CA
21 December 2015